ICE AGE

Contents

Ice Age Hunters — page 2

Ag and the Snow Sticks — page 12

Alison Hawes

Story illustrated by Pet Gotohda

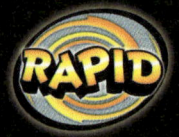# Before Reading

Find out about

- Ice Age hunters and the animals they killed

Tricky words

- thousands
- pictures
- painted
- spears
- deer
- woolly mammoth
- sabre-tooth tiger

Introduce these tricky words and help the reader when they come across them later!

Text starter

Ice Age hunters lived in caves thousands of years ago. They hunted small animals like deer and big animals like woolly mammoths.

Ice Age Hunters

Ice Age hunters lived thousands of years ago.
They lived in caves.

Cave pictures

Ice Age hunters painted pictures on the walls of their caves.

They painted pictures of the animals they hunted.

The pictures show how the Ice Age hunters killed the animals.

The Ice Age hunters made spears with sticks and stones.

Hunting small animals

Ice Age hunters killed small animals like deer.

They killed the deer with their spears.

They dragged the deer to their caves.

Then they cooked the meat.

Hunting big animals

Ice Age hunters killed big animals like the woolly mammoth.

A woolly mammoth was like a big hairy elephant.

They trapped the woolly mammoth in a pit.

Then they killed it with their spears.

They cut up the woolly mammoth.

Then they cooked the meat.

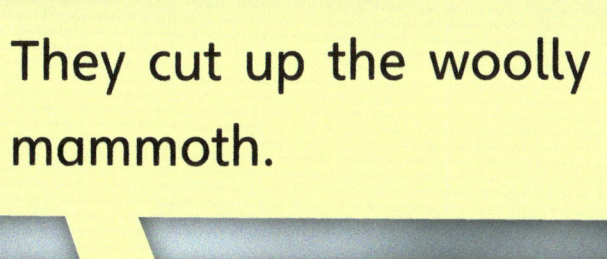

Ice Age hunters killed sabre-tooth tigers with their spears.

Quiz

Text Detective

- What animals did Ice Age people hunt?
- Would you like to live in a cave?

Word Detective

- **Phonic Focus:** Blending three phonemes
  Page 8: Can you sound out 'pit'?
  What is the sound in the middle?
- Page 6: Find a word which is the opposite of 'big'.
- Page 5: Find a word to rhyme with 'bones'.

Super Speller

Read these words:

with   like   made

Now try to spell them!

HA! HA! HA!

Q What do woolly mammoths wear to go swimming?

A Their trunks!

Before Reading

In this story

 Ag

 Rocky

Tricky words

- wanted
- woolly mammoth
- spear
- Snow Sticks
- fast
- catch
- after

Introduce these tricky words and help the reader when they come across them later!

Story starter

Ag and her big brother Rocky are cave people who lived long ago. Ag is full of good ideas to make their lives more comfortable, but Rocky laughs at her ideas – he's so sure they will never catch on! One day, Ag and Rocky wanted to go hunting for a woolly mammoth.

Ag and the Snow Sticks

Rocky wanted to hunt a woolly mammoth.
So he got his hunting spear.

Ag wanted to go hunting too.

So she got her hunting spear and then she put some sticks on her feet.

"**What** is on your feet?" said Rocky.

"Snow Sticks," said Ag.

"Snow Sticks are silly!" said Rocky.

But Ag's Snow Sticks went fast in the snow.

Rocky ran to catch up with her.

Then Rocky and Ag saw a woolly mammoth.

"Run and catch it!" said Ag.

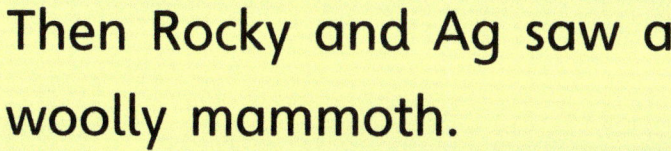

So Rocky got his spear and went after the woolly mammoth.

But the woolly mammoth saw Rocky and ran away.

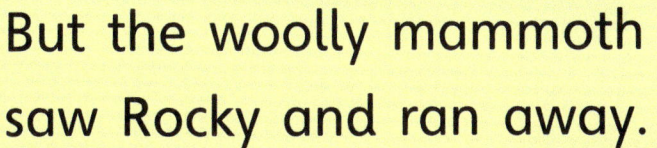

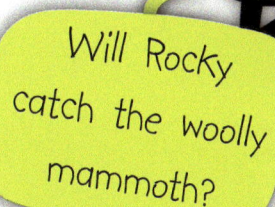

Will Rocky catch the woolly mammoth?

"Put on my Snow Sticks!" said Ag. "My Snow Sticks go fast in the snow."

Rocky went too fast on the Snow Sticks.

He hit a tree!

"I said your Snow Sticks are silly," said Rocky. "Snow Sticks will **never** catch on!"

Quiz

Text Detective

- Why did Ag put Snow Sticks on her feet?
- Have Snow Sticks caught on?

Word Detective

- **Phonic Focus:** Blending three phonemes Pages 17 and 19: Sound out 'run' and 'ran'. What is different?
- Page 15: Why is 'what' in bold print?
- Page 20: Find a word that means 'quickly'.

Super Speller

Read these words:

fast   will   your

Now try to spell them!

HA! HA! HA!

Q Where do you find woolly mammoths?

A It depends on where you've left them!